WOULD YOU RATHER ??

FOR KIDS

WOULD YOU RATHER...?

Be able to fly?

- OR -

Be able to turn invisible?

- OR -

Have super-strength?

WOULD YOU RATHER...?

Go 3 days without water?

- OR -

Go two weeks without food?

- OR -

Go five days without sleep?

WOULD YOU RATHER...?

Burp flames?

- OR -

Sneeze electricity?

- OR -

Cough lasers?

WOULD YOU RATHER...?

Sleep with the fishes?

- OR -

Snooze with the whales?

- OR -

Nap with the sea turtles?

WOULD YOU RATHER...?

Be trapped inside a bookstore?

- OR -

Be trapped inside a videogame store?

- OR -

c. Be trapped inside a candy store?

WOULD YOU RATHER...?

Be the best finder at hide-and-seek?

- OR -

Be the best hider in hide-and-seek?

- OR -

Be okay at both?

WOULD YOU RATHER...?

Read people's minds?

- OR -

Feel what others feel?

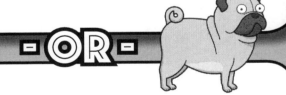

- OR -

Tell someone else's future?

WOULD YOU RATHER...?

Never be able to use your phone again?

 OR

Have to hold your phone for the rest of your life?

 OR

Only be able to use your phone when standing on your head?

WOULD YOU RATHER...?

Have a monkey tail?

- OR -

Have crocodile teeth?

- OR -

Have eagle wings?

WOULD YOU RATHER...?

Lose your sense of sight?

 OR

Lose your sense of hearing?

 OR

Lose your sense of feeling?

WOULD YOU RATHER...?

Only eat red foods?

Only eat yellow foods?

Only eat orange foods?

WOULD YOU RATHER...?

Have lettuce for hands?

- OR -

Have carrots for teeth?

- OR -

Have celery for toes?

WOULD YOU RATHER...?

Only communicate with
your toes?

- OR -

Only communicate with
your hands?

- OR -

Only communicate with
your lips?

WOULD YOU RATHER...?

Only be able to wear the color grey?

-OR-

Only be able to wear the color black?

-OR-

Only be able to wear the color white?

WOULD YOU RATHER...?

Turn people into a random animal when you say their name?

- OR -

be turned into a random animal when people say your name?

- OR -

or turn into a random animal when you hear your own name?

WOULD YOU RATHER...?

Be able to change your height at will?

Be able to change your weight at will?

Be able to change your appearance at will?

WOULD YOU RATHER...?

Have Aladdin's magic carpet?

- OR -

Have Cinderella's pumpkin coach?

- OR -

Own a unicorn?

WOULD YOU RATHER...?

Be 2 foot taller than you are now?

-OR-

Be two foot shorter than you are now?

-OR-

Randomly become either ten inches taller or ten inches shorter than you? are now?

WOULD YOU RATHER...?

Be able to turn back time

 - OR -

Be able to make time stand still?

- OR -

Be able to speed time up?

WOULD YOU RATHER...?

Go anywhere in your country whenever you want?

 - OR -

Be able to travel to any country within an hour

- OR -

Have a magical airplane that could bring anyone to you whenever you want?

WOULD YOU RATHER...?

Eat only strawberries? Eat only strawberries?

- OR -

Eat only blueberries?

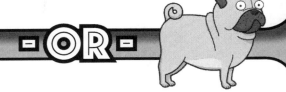

- OR -

Eat only raspberries?

WOULD YOU RATHER...?

Meet all your ancestors from the past?

 OR

Meet all your descendants in the future?

 OR

Meet all your distant cousins?

WOULD YOU RATHER...?

Only be able to speak in rhyme?

- OR -

Only be able to speak in song?

- OR -

Only be able to speak with a funny accent?

WOULD YOU RATHER...?

Live where it's always hot?

- OR -

Live where it's always cold?

- OR -

Live where it always rains?

WOULD YOU RATHER...?

listen to music?

- OR -

read poetry?

- OR -

look at art?

WOULD YOU RATHER...?

Only be able to call people by their last name?

 OR

Only be able to call people by "sir" or "ma'am?"

 OR

Only be able to address people by "quack!" or "moo!"?

WOULD YOU RATHER...?

Never eat chocolate again?

- OR -

Never eat cheese again?

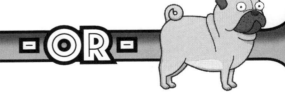

- OR -

Never eat bread again?

WOULD YOU RATHER...?

Travel by bus?

- OR -

Travel by train

 - OR -

Travel by plane?

WOULD YOU RATHER...?

Read a book?

- OR -

Watch a movie?

- OR -

Watch TV?

WOULD YOU RATHER...?

Sleep on your stomach for the rest of your life?

OR

Sleep on your side for the rest of your life?

OR

Sleep on your back for the rest of your life?

WOULD YOU RATHER...?

Lose the ability to see the color red?

- OR -

Lose the ability to see the color blue?

- OR -

Lose the ability to see the color yellow?

WOULD YOU RATHER...?

Read peoples minds when you're near them?

- OR -

Read one other person mind from any distance?

- OR -

Read all the peoples mind you've ever spoken to from five miles away?

WOULD YOU RATHER...?

Burp every time you met someone?

- OR -

Sneeze every time you shook someone's hand?

- OR -

Cough every time someone says your name?

WOULD YOU RATHER...?

Be the smartest person in the world?

 -OR-

Be the most athletic person in the world?

 -OR-

Be the most attractive person in the world?

WOULD YOU RATHER...?

Turn on & off all the lights in the building whenever you blinked?

- OR -

Turn on all the water in the building whenever you inhaled?

- OR -

Unlock all the doors in the building whenever you exhaled?

WOULD YOU RATHER...?

Spend your weekend alone?

- OR -

Spend your weekend with a lot of people?

- OR -

Spend your weekend with one person?

WOULD YOU RATHER...?

Only text Bitmojis?

Only email emojis?

Only post on social media in gifs?

WOULD YOU RATHER...?

Relax at the beach?

- OR -

Explore in the mountains?

- OR -

Check out a new city?

WOULD YOU RATHER...?

Lose the ability to tie your shoes?

- OR -

Lose the ability to zipper your pants?

- OR -

Lose the ability to button your shirt?

WOULD YOU RATHER...?

Control your hair color at will?

-OR-

Control your hair's shape at will?

-OR-

Control your hair's length at will?

WOULD YOU RATHER...?

Get stuck in an elevator?

- OR -

Get lost in the forest?

- OR -

Have your pants stuck in an escalator?

WOULD YOU RATHER...?

Have never ending body odor?

- OR -

Have never ending bad breath?

- OR -

Always have something in your teeth?

WOULD YOU RATHER...?

Cause an earthquake whenever you laughed?

= OR =

Cause a tsunami whenever you cried

= OR =

Cause a tornado whenever you yawned?

WOULD YOU RATHER...?

Be Iron Man?

Be Captain America?

OR

Be Thor?

WOULD YOU RATHER...?

Leave purple handprints on everything you touch?

- OR -

Leave orange footprints wherever you walk?

- OR -

Flash lasers at everything you look at?

WOULD YOU RATHER...?

Own a rocket ship?

Own a speedboat?

Own an airplane?

WOULD YOU RATHER....?

Be a lion tamer?

- OR -

Be a snake charmer?

- OR -

Be a horse whisperer?

WOULD YOU RATHER...?

Have dinner with a past president?

- OR -

Have dinner with the current president?

- OR -

Have dinner with the next president?

WOULD YOU RATHER...?

Eat a pancake without syrup?

- OR -

Eat French fries without ketchup?

- OR -

Eat spaghetti without sauce?

WOULD YOU RATHER....?

Be a kid forever?

- OR -

Be an adult forever?

- OR -

Be a teen forever?

WOULD YOU RATHER...?

Have farts that smell like hot dogs?

- OR -

Have burps that smell like hamburgers?

- OR -

Have body odor that smells like pizza

WOULD YOU RATHER...?

Have your nose grow whenever you told a lie?

 -OR-

Grow an inch every time you broke a promise?

 -OR-

Have your ears grow whenever someone lied to you?

WOULD YOU RATHER...?

See your own funeral?

- OR -

See your own birth?

- OR -

Relive one random birthday?

WOULD YOU RATHER...?

Only eat fruity candy?

OR

Only eat chocolate candy?

OR

Only eat mint candy (including gum)?

WOULD YOU RATHER...?

Misplace your wallet?

- OR -

Misplace your keys?

- OR -

Misplace your phone?

WOULD YOU RATHER...?

Turn into a dog?

 OR

Turn into a cat?

 OR

Turn into a bird?

WOULD YOU RATHER...?

Visit Europe?

- OR -

Visit Asia?

- OR -

Visit Africa?

WOULD YOU RATHER...?

Eat whatever you want?

- OR -

Have perfect health?

- OR -

Be physically fit?

WOULD YOU RATHER....?

Win one billion dollars?

- OR -

Live for two hundred years?

- OR -

Not age, but live a normal amount of time?

WOULD YOU RATHER...?

Have nice arm muscles?

-OR-

Have nice abdomen muscles?

-OR-

Have nice leg muscles?

WOULD YOU RATHER...?

Control the weather?

- OR -

Control electricity?

- OR -

Control gravity?

WOULD YOU RATHER...?

Have a party with all your friends?

-OR-

Have a party with all your family?

-OR-

Have a party with half your friends and half your family?

WOULD YOU RATHER...?

be able to speak, but not understand, any language?

 - OR -

be able to understand, but not speak, any language?

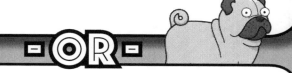 - OR -

Be able to understand half of all languages, and speak the other half?

WOULD YOU RATHER...?

Be able to control gravity on yourself?

▪️◉®◉▪️ OR ▪️◉®◉▪️

Be able to control gravity on objects

▪️◉®◉▪️ OR ▪️◉®◉▪️

Be able to control gravity on other people?

WOULD YOU RATHER...?

See into the past, but only where you're standing?

- OR -

Travel anywhere in the world instantly

- OR -

See into the future, but only where you're standing?

WOULD YOU RATHER...?

Control the wind?

-OR-

Control the temperature?

-OR-

Control the Humidity?

WOULD YOU RATHER...?

Have hands for feet?

- OR -

Have feet for hands?

- OR -

Have your hands and feet in their normal spots, but with your arms and legs switched?

WOULD YOU RATHER...?

Have super sticky hands?

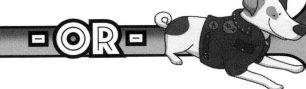 OR

Have super slippery hands?

 OR

Have super magnetic hands?

WOULD YOU RATHER...?

Be a famous actor?

- OR -

Be a famous athlete?

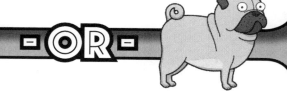

- OR -

Be a famous singer?

WOULD YOU RATHER...?

Be able to speak to animals?

- **OR** -

Be able to talk to machines?

- **OR** -

Be able to communicate in any language?

WOULD YOU RATHER...?

Be stranded in the desert alone?

Be stranded in the desert with someone you don't like?

Be stranded in the desert with someone who doesn't speak the same language as you?

WOULD YOU RATHER...?

Eat the same dinner every day?

- OR -

Eat the same lunch every day?

- OR -

Eat the same breakfast every day?

WOULD YOU RATHER...?

Have a dishwasher?

- OR -

Have a washing machine?

- OR -

Have central air conditioning?

WOULD YOU RATHER...?

Have unlimited time?

-OR-

Have unlimited money?

-OR-

Have unlimited brain power?

Made in the USA
Middletown, DE
08 February 2023

24248813R00042